Real Life GUIDES

TRAVEL & TOURISM

REAL LIFE GUIDES

Practical guides for practical people

In this series of career guides from Trotman, we look in detail at what it takes to train for, get into and be successful at a wide spectrum of practical careers. The *Real Life Guides* aim to inform and inspire young people and adults alike by providing comprehensive yet hard-hitting and often blunt information about what it takes to succeed in these careers.

Other titles in this series are:

Real Life Guides: The Armed Forces
Real Life Guides: The Beauty Industry, 2nd edition
Real Life Guides: Care
Real Life Guides: Carpentry & Cabinet-Making, 2nd edition
Real Life Guides: Catering, 2nd edition
Real Life Guides: Construction, 2nd edition
Real Life Guides: Distribution & Logistics
Real Life Guides: Electrician, 2nd edition
Real Life Guides: Engineering Technician
Real Life Guides: The Fire Service
Real Life Guides: Hairdressing, 2nd edition
Real Life Guides: Information & Communications Technology
Real Life Guides: The Motor Industry, 2nd edition
Real Life Guides: Passenger Transport
Real Life Guides: Plumbing, 2nd edition
Real Life Guides: The Police Force
Real Life Guides: Retail, 2nd edition
Real Life Guides: Transport
Real Life Guides: Travel & Tourism
Real Life Guides: Working Outdoors, 2nd edition
Real Life Guides: Working with Animals & Wildlife, 2nd edition
Real Life Guides: Working with Young People

trotman

Real
Life
GUIDES

TRAVEL & TOURISM

Sara Evans

Real Life Guides: Travel & Tourism

This first edition published in 2008 by Trotman Publishing,
a division of Crimson Publishing Ltd., Westminster House,
Kew Road, Richmond, Surrey TW9 2ND

Author Sara Evans

British Library Cataloguing in Publication Data

A catalogue record for this book is available from the British
Library

ISBN 978 1 84455 171 2

Typeset by RefineCatch Ltd, Bungay, Suffolk

Printed and bound in Great Britain by Athenaeum Press,
Gateshead

Real Life

GUIDES

CONTENTS

About the author

Sara Evans is an award-winning freelance journalist specialising in travel, education and wildlife. Her articles and photographs have been published in broadsheet newspapers and magazines in both the UK and abroad. Sara also works as the Head of Content on a leading online service for schools focusing on providing careers education for 11 to 18 year olds. She is the author of *The Travel Industry Uncovered*, a careers guide published by Trotman.

Dedicated to my son, Jacob

Foreword

Foreword

If you are energetic, enjoy working with people and have a passion for adventure, travel and tourism could be the job for you. This fun but often hard-working industry offers a broad range of opportunities and City & Guilds provides a variety of qualifications that make sure you'll be ready for your first day.

As a leading provider of vocational qualifications, awarding over 1 million certificates every year, City & Guilds offers over 500 qualifications at all levels. These range from basic skills and pre-entry qualifications to awards that recognise professional achievement at the highest levels. Their qualifications are available in over 100 countries and are recognised by employers worldwide as proof of the knowledge and skills needed to get the job done.

City & Guilds is delighted to be part of the Trotman *Real Life Guides* series to help raise your awareness of these vocational qualifications. If travel and tourism is for you, all you need is the right training, so for more information about the courses City & Guilds offers check out www.cityand guilds.com and you could be meeting interesting people from all over the world sooner than you think.

Introduction

Travel and tourism – just saying the words out loud stirs the imagination in most people. Visions of white beaches, turquoise seas and cloudless skies usually tend to appear first. But while a career in travel and tourism may involve some time in exotic and beautiful locations, for most people working in the sector the experience is rather different.

The jobs in travel and tourism are varied, but almost all demand dedication, long hours and a flexible approach to working. Working as a member of a Cabin Crew team aboard a plane may well take you to some glamorous destinations, but you may find you have little time to spend there or are too tired to take advantage of where you are. Having said this, though, most people in the sector find their jobs rewarding and satisfying.

They love working with people and helping them – through all sorts of ways – find the best travel and holiday experience they can possibly have. And with the sector being the fastest growing one around the world, the demand for travel and tourism experiences looks unlikely to go away. In fact, people want more holidays and they

DID YOU KNOW THAT?

- Over 2 million jobs are sustained by tourism activity in the UK, either directly or indirectly
- There are an estimated 1.45 million jobs directly related to tourism activity in the UK, some 5% of all people in employment in the UK
- Approximately 132,400 of these jobs are in self-employment.

Source: Visit Britain

want them to be green, they want to book them online and whether these trips are UK based or half away across the globe, these experiences must be unforgettable.

Which is where you come in: in whatever role suits you best, advising, planning and booking a dream vacation or, once in their new location, supporting the traveller and ensuring that all goes smoothly until the guest returns home.

DID YOU KNOW?

- Tourism is the largest and fastest growing industry in the world
- In 2000, there were nearly 700 million tourists, and in 2020, it's predicted, there will be around 1.6 billion.

Source: WWF

The rest of this book looks at the sort of jobs that are available. From Theme Park Workers to Tour Operators, you'll find out the skills and qualifications required, likely hours, rates of pay and prospects for the future. There are also quizzes to help you find out what role might be right for you as well as action plans which suggest helpful activities that will provide you with some relevant experiences to add weight to your CV.

Dip in and out of this book or read from cover-to-cover to find out if a travel and tourism career is for you. And, if you find that it is, then follow the helpful hints and tips to actually get the job you want. Good luck and enjoy the journey!

JESSIE TODD

Case study 1

**ASSISTANT MANAGER
OF A TRAVEL AGENT**

*Starting as an apprentice with
a well-known travel agent, Jessie Todd
went on to become an assistant manager
and has travelled to some very exciting
places. Find out here, how Jessie's career
has gone from strength to strength...*

When Jessie left school at 16 with
a good selection of GCSEs she had no
idea what career path to follow. Little
did Jessie know that over the next few
years her eventual job would take her
to countries as exotic and exciting as
Morocco, Barbados and Egypt.

Although Jessie enjoyed learning, she
didn't want to stay on at school to take
A Levels and then go on to study further at
university. She explains, 'I'm quite hands on
and was keen on earning rather than going
to university and ending up with debts'.

Still not knowing what exactly to do –
but knowing she didn't want to study
further – Jessie had a lucky break. Just
walking down her local high street a poster
attached to a shop window seemed to
jump out at her. The shop was a travel
agent (Thomson) and the poster was

> I loved the
> whole programme
> of learning and
> earning at my
> own pace.

asking young people to consider becoming an apprentice in the travel industry.

Intrigued, Jessie went into Thomson and found out a little more about the opportunity. She then sent off an application form. Jessie was invited to attend an interview and also experienced a taster day to get a real feel of what working in a travel agent's would be like. Once the apprenticeship started, Jessie knew she had made the right decision.

'I loved the whole programme of learning and earning at my own pace. The money wasn't amazing at the beginning but I knew once I was trained there were good career prospects and the money would improve,' says Jessie.

Enjoying the programme, Jessie was one of the first to complete her NVQ 2 and was then fast-tracked onto NVQ 3 – which she also finished quickly. In fact, Jessie's achievements, hard work and commitment were so impressive that she was awarded Personal Achiever of the Year at the 2006 Apprenticeship Awards.

And since her award, Jessie's career has continued to flourish. From starting as an apprentice, she has gone to become the assistant manager at another branch of Thomson. Jessie still sells holidays, but also has responsibility for the smooth running of the office, staff training and team talks.

Not only this, but Jessie was also offered the opportunity to study for a foundation degree. She says, 'It will mean studying for a further three years, but it will be funded by the company. I'm really happy with my job now – with or without a degree – but I know this could open even more doors up to higher management and that's exciting.'

What's the story?

So a travel and tourism career certainly sounds interesting, but what's the job security like and is it an industry that can stand up to the rigours of the credit crunch? This chapter takes a look at the employment trends of the industry and considers the prospects for the future.

GOOD OUTLOOK

With budget airlines and online booking making overseas trips increasingly accessible and Britain continuing to attract increasing numbers to its shores, opportunities to work at the heart of travel and tourism both home and abroad continue to rise.

Over 120,000 people currently work within the British tourism industry; and whether it's a distinct travel or tourism role with a large commercial company, or with one of the smaller enterprises, or a supporting role such as marketing or IT– with the right skills, experience and qualifications you should be able to find an available role to suit you.

UK PROSPECTS

Many people assume that working in travel and tourism means you'll be based overseas. This just isn't the case. There are plenty of opportunities to have a successful travel and tourism career without leaving British shores. The UK, with its rich heritage, beautiful coastlines, traditional sporting events (such as Wimbledon) and vibrant cities continues to attract visitors from all the over the world. With London hosting the 2012 Olympics, the demand for travel and tourism services is estimated to be sky high – an excellent opportunity to find work or gain experience in the sector.

TRAVEL FACTS

- In 2000, across the global economy, travel and tourism accounted for around 11% of world exports, goods and services, surpassing trade in food, textiles, and chemicals.
- Around 15 million people from the UK go on package holidays every year. That's roughly 30 holidaymakers jetting-off every minute of every day.
- The Mediterranean is the world's most popular holiday destination. More than 11 million British people visit the region every year.
- Nearly 80% of international tourists come from Europe and the Americas, while only 15% come from East Asia and the Pacific, and 5% from Africa, the Middle East and South Asia.
- In the UK, 80% of all holidaymakers are carried by four big tour operators.

Source: WWF

OPPORTUNITIES ABROAD

Budget air travel and online booking has revolutionised the way people holiday – it's boosted the number of people travelling abroad and increased demand for services to support them once away from home. As well as providing more opportunities for domestic call centre and internet work, more people have been required to work, for example, as tour guides and holiday representatives abroad. And increasingly, holidaymakers expect their representatives and guides to be specialists in the areas in which they work. Language and communication skills have never been more important and detailed knowledge of a specific region or country been more highly valued.

Home or away: key areas where you can spread your wings.

- **Tour operators:** whether it's the big name companies offering instant fun in the sun or the smaller specialist promising more unusual experiences (everything from working holidays on African wildlife reserves to dedicated water sports breaks), there are plenty of roles needed to keep operators in business; think marketing, operations, sales, administration, IT, contracts and product development. There are also more opportunities available 'on site' at hotels and resorts for reps.
- **Travel agencies:** the lure of the push-button PC holiday doesn't sit comfortably with many people, meaning that the traditional high street travel agency still has a significant role to play in the industry. Like operators, agencies can also specialise in less well-known destinations providing far-away soul-enriching volunteering opportunities for the customer not interested in a traditional package break. Some agencies also specialise

in arranging business travel. Sales and administration roles dominate in this bastion of the great British escape.

- **Ground handlers:** whether you choose to stay home and welcome tourists into your home town or fly off to exercise your foreign language skills in Europe, careers on the ground are the backbone of global tourism; think hoteliers, tour guides, waiting staff, chefs, water-park instructors, wildlife rangers, museum curators and retail assistants.

- **Tourist information centres:** the first point of call for the bewildered UK or international visitor, tourist information centres offer great opportunities for those with strong customer service skills. And you don't see many tourist information centres shutting down, do you?

- **Tourism consultancies:** in the age of the consultancy where research is, for example, conducted to predict travel and tourism trends, the demand for people with finance, IT and marketing ambitions or qualifications is growing. Interesting behind-the-scenes opportunities exist here.

- **Eco-tourism:** this is the word on the lips of many people working in the travel and tourism industry. Green holidays, ways to reduce carbon footprints and benefiting local people and communities are at the forefront of many holiday itineraries. And as the world starts to pay more and more attention to the threat of global warming and the injustices of third world poverty, it's a subset of the industry that is predicted to grow.

OVERALL PROSPECTS

The forecast is sunny for the travel and tourism industry despite the threats from terrorism and global recession. The World Travel and Tourism Council's (WTTC) 'new tourism' blueprint has advised governments that leaving tourism 'to chance' is no longer acceptable and 'sustainability' – which positively impacts upon local jobs, livelihoods and the environment – must always be at the forefront of their strategies.

Travel and tourism is a sector that continues to grow and one which is taken increasingly seriously since its impact is far reaching both nationally and globally. If you want to be part of such an industry move on to the next chapter to find out more about the work that could get you involved in a sector that's really going places.

GUIDE TO TRAVEL AND TOURISM JARGON

- **Incoming or inbound tourism:** visitors coming to the UK from other countries
- **Outbound tourism:** UK residents leaving the UK to travel abroad
- **Domestic tourism:** residents in the UK travelling in the UK
- **Ecotourism:** the International Ecotourism Society describes this as 'responsible travel to natural areas that conserves the environment and sustains the well-being of local people'
- **FITs:** stands for 'fully independent travellers' – basically travellers who follow their own itinerary rather than in an organised package or tour

- **GITs:** stands for 'group independent travellers' – a group of people who follow their own itinerary without a tour guide
- **Ground handlers:** tour operators who provide services to incoming passengers
- **Long haul:** faraway destinations such as the Middle East, East and South-East Asia and the Americas
- **Sustainable tourism:** the World Tourism Organisation (UNWTO) describes this as practice which 'meets the needs of the present tourists and host regions while protecting and enhancing the opportunity for the future. It is envisaged as leading to management of all resources in such a way that economic, social and aesthetic needs can be fulfilled, while maintaining cultural integrity, essential ecological processes, biological diversity and life support systems'
- **TICs:** tourist information centres
- **VFR:** the domestic trend of travelling to visit friends and relatives.

Source: Prospects

The jobs

The types of jobs on offer in the travel and tourism sector
are as wide and varied as they are interesting. In this
chapter, you will find an overview of the main jobs available.

AIR CABIN CREW

Working on planes, Air Cabin Crew work directly with
passengers ensuring they have safe, comfortable and
pleasant flights. Main duties include:

- Keeping the plane clean and tidy
- Checking the plane is stocked with the right medical
  supplies
- Checking the plane is carrying enough food and drink
- Ensuring cabin equipment is all in order
- Overseeing passengers boarding the plane
- Selling duty free items/gifts
- Serving meals and drinks to passengers during flights.

CRUISE SHIP WORK

Working on a cruise ship, holiday representatives are
responsible for passengers who have booked their passages
with their holiday company. Typical duties are as follows:

- Meeting passengers portside and ensuring that cabins
  are found
- Holding onboard welcome meeting
- Providing support and information regarding itineraries at
  ports of call
- Selling tours and activities at ports of call
- Answering any questions regarding the cruise

- Assisting guests who become ill or experience problems (such as lost passports)
- Ensuring guests are happy with their cabin and onboard activities and services.

COACH TOUR OPERATOR

Coach Tour Operators specialise in putting together holiday packages which rely on travelling by coach as the sole or main source of transport. In the main, coach tour operators:

- Put together itineraries for either UK or international coach tours
- Plan, research, visit and check venues, hotels etc that will be visited during a tour
- Develop and improve existing coach tour packages
- Negotiate costs and bookings with coach companies (if not working directly for a coach company), hoteliers and venues
- Liaise with coach companies, hoteliers and venues to ensure operations are run as scheduled
- Create marketing material promoting coach tours.

HOLIDAY REPRESENTATIVE

Working for a holiday company, Holiday Representatives – or Reps as they are more commonly known – are responsible for looking after holiday-makers at particular resorts. Reps are usually involved in:

- Meeting guests at airports, taking them to their accommodation and checking they are happy with their accommodation
- Running induction meetings and providing them with information regarding their resort and the surrounding area
- Selling trips, tours and excursions
- Assisting guests with local transport and equipment hire and currency exchange
- Dealing with any complaints or issues that guests may have regarding their holiday
- Managing paperwork regarding any complaints, accidents or noteworthy incidents.

HOLIDAY CENTRE WORK

Work in a holiday centre varies from one centre to another. Duties, though, tend to focus around the following areas:

- Cleaning and housekeeping
- Catering – such as waiting, staffing bars and simple food preparation
- Guest services – such as reception work or shop work
- Activities – organising social events and games (think bingo and dancing nights).

THEME PARK ASSISTANT

Based in a theme park, Assistants look after visitors ensuring they have a fun day out and may help maintain the park to ensure its safety. Theme Park Assistants tend to:

- Carry out safety checks
- Operate and supervise rides
- Make small repairs
- Undertake light cleaning duties

- Ensure that visitors keep hold of their personal belongings
  Sell merchandise or light refreshments
- Make announcements and advertise attractions and rides.

TOUR GUIDE
Accompanying visitors to tourist attractions and sites
(including cities, buildings, heritage sites and museums
in the UK or abroad), the work of a Tour Guide includes:

- Passing on detailed information regarding a site's history,
  geography and purpose etc
- Answering visitors' questions and directing them to
  related places of interest if appropriate.

TOUR MANAGER
Tour Managers make the arrangements for groups of
holidaymakers and ensure that these arrangements run
smoothly for the duration of the trip. Typical duties include:

- Joining holidaymakers at the start of their holiday/journey
- Welcoming the party, checking tickets and providing
  itinerary information
- Providing ongoing commentary during the trip on places
  of interest as well as local history, life and culture
- Checking arrangements and confirming ongoing travel
  arrangements
- Sorting out problems and keeping records relating to
  the trip.

TOURIST INFORMATION CENTRE ASSISTANT
Assistants working in tourist information centres provide
information based on their knowledge of the local area to
tourists. They also:

- Book accommodation and places on trips or tours
- Provide directions and answer queries from visitors using the internet and/or printed materials
- Prepare and send out mailshots
- Sell souvenirs and postcards.

TRANSFER REPRESENTATIVE

Representing individual holiday and travel companies, Transfer Representatives:

- Receive and welcomes guests at airports
- Ensure these guests have a smooth transfer to their accommodation
- At the end of a tour/holiday, Transfer Representatives ensure guests return to their airport on time for the next leg of their journey.

TRAVEL AGENT SALES CONSULTANT

Often referred to just as travel agents, Travel Agent Sales Consultants promote and sell holidays. Typical activities include:

- Selling and booking holiday packages
- Selling and booking airline tickets
- Arranging car hire and currency exchange
- Administrative and record keeping activities.

DID YOU KNOW?

That there are more travel agents in the travel and tourism industry than any other role — for example:

- 40% of the workforce are travel agents
- 6% are travel agency managers
- 9% are travel or tour guides
- The other roles are mainly in related areas such as customer care, marketing and administration.

Source: Labour Force Survey, 2004q2– 2005q1

RATHER WRITE ABOUT TRAVEL THAN SELL IT?

Travel writing and photography have very glamorous associations. The popular image is of a journalist or photographer spending time in beautiful locations and staying in luxurious accommodation for a few weeks (all paid for) and then writing up a story or processing photographs to sell to waiting newspapers and magazines for hefty fees.

Reality, though, is rather different. First, few publications these days pay for writers to travel to their destinations. Secondly, the time spent at a destination can be minimal, and thirdly it is a highly competitive industry where getting published can be very difficult and not necessarily financially rewarding.

However, if you are prepared to make sacrifices and to keep trying, you may be one of the lucky ones who gets to see their work in print. Many travel writers are trained journalists so getting related qualifications can be helpful. Contact the National Council for the Training of Journalists (www.nctj.com) for more information on courses.

Now move onto the next chapter which provides you with an insight into the type of skills and personal qualities needed by people who work in travel and tourism. To find out more about the salaries, typical working conditions and entry requirements associated with the jobs above, check out the FAQs chapter on page 34.

QUIZ

Find out if a career in travel and tourism could suit you by answering the quiz questions below:

When you've been on holiday with the school, how often do you call home?

   a. Once – I'm too busy having fun!
   b. About three times, I can't help thinking about my family
   c. Every single day, I suffer terribly from homesickness

How do you feel about working at night, catching up on zeds in the day?

   a. Fine, I'm a night owl anyway
   b. It's far from ideal but I'm sure I'll get used to it
   c. You're kidding? I'd fall asleep on the job!

You've got a stinking cold but are strapped for cash and are forced to go into your Saturday job in a shop. An awkward customer keeps changing their mind about buying a particular item. How do you react to them?

   a. I make an effort to help them decide
   b. Smile through gritted teeth
   c. Tell them you'll be back in two hours when they've made their choice

Your friend from America comes to visit in the summer. What do you do on your first day?

   a. See the sights
   b. Go shopping
   c. Go to the cinema

Can you speak another language?

    a. Yes, I am taking a language at A Level
    b. Conversational, yes, I took a language at GCSE
    c. I can say hello in a few European languages

How interested are you in world geography?

    a. Name a country, and I'll tell you the capital
    b. I adore reading travel literature
    c. I am more interested in visiting these places than reading about them

Which of these ways of working suits you best?

    a. Being on my feet all day and busy
    b. Being behind a wheel once I can drive!
    c. Sitting behind a state-of-the-art desk

Which of these attributes are your friends most likely to attribute to you?

    a. Gets on with people from all walks of life, and all ages
    b. Is punctual and reliable
    c. Is always up for a laugh

Your friend tells you he/she is going to Florida next year. What are you feeling inside?

    a. I'll go there one day, it'll be amazing!
    b. Wish it was me … I hope they bring me a present!
    c. I can't believe I never get to go abroad … it's so UNFAIR!

Do you enjoy working on a PC?

   a. I love it – bit of an addict really!
   b. Yeah, but too much and my eyes go googly!
   c. No, what ever happened to good old fashioned handwriting?

A tourist stops you on the street and asks you where the best place to visit is in your city. What do you say?

   a. You reveal the top three attractions and tell them exactly how to get there
   b. Point them in the direction of the tourist information office
   c. Tell them you're really not sure, you'd hate to offer them bad advice!

Now add up how many As, Bs or Cs you have selected and match to the info below.

Mostly As – wow! A career in travel and tourism could be so right for you. With your flexible approach to life, cheerful attitude and keenness to help others you should definitely check out the whole range of jobs that are available – there will certainly be one that matches your career aspirations in the sector.

Mostly Bs – not bad! You seem to be in with a good chance of finding some travel and tourism work that could be right for you. You may not be suited to every role in the sector but there should be something that grabs your fancy and suits your character. Sift through our job descriptions on p. 11 to find something that floats your boat.

Mostly Cs – mmm… a career in travel and tourism may not, at first sight, seem to be the thing for you. To work successfully in this sector, you really need to be able to combine a love of the world and travel with a strong urge to help others enjoy the same. However, there are lots of roles that are connected with the industry – such as accounting and marketing – that may suit you nicely. Why not check them out?

OTHER RELATED JOBS IN TRAVEL AND TOURISM

As well as the jobs looked at in this chapter, there are lots of other related jobs in the sector that may be of interest. Typical areas include:

- **Marketing:** this is a key area important for attracting new customers and showcasing new holidays and tours. As well as exposure in print, online marketing is big business too
- **IT:** the industry relies heavily on IT specialists for electronic booking, databases, office systems and websites
- **Accounts:** accountants are needed by all sizes and sorts of companies operating in the sector
- **Customer and legal services:** these skills are needed to ensure customer loyalty and avoid the making of costly legal mistakes.

Tools of the trade

Careers in the travel and tourism industry are varied and exciting but they all involve working with people – be they based in the UK or abroad. So, as you might expect, the skills and qualities needed to work in them tend to be people-focused.

In this chapter we take a closer look at these skills and qualities. There are also a couple of quizzes to help you see if you have got the skills and qualities needed for a career in travel and tourism.

THE SKILLS

● **Customer service skills:** people-facing skills are very highly considered in the travel and tourism industry. Why? Well, since the sector is all about keeping people happy – whether on their holidays or spending the day at a theme park – it is important that they are dealt with respectively and thoughtfully. If they aren't, then they may not come back to the theme park or choose to book next year's holiday with another company.

● **Organisation:** being able to organise your day as well as other people's is an important skill in this sector. For example, as a Holiday Representative you need to turn up on time to your guest meetings and have all the paperwork you need to hand out with you. Travel Agents need to be sure they book all the correct tickets and ensure that they get to their clients on time.

- **Communication:** related to customer service skills, communication is also a very important skill. If you are working as a Tour Guide, for example, you will need to pass on facts in a clear and interesting way. Holiday Centre and Cruise Ship Workers need to be able to communicate effectively with their clients so they are clear what a day's activities may involve.
- **Tact and diplomacy:** being able to deal with tricky situations in a sensitive and polite way can be a very helpful and is also considered a people-facing skill. Dealing with a nervous and irrational passenger on a plane requires diplomacy by Cabin Crew Staff as does dealing with an angry client on a coach tour. Not dealing with clients in this way could, for example, lead to the nervous flyer becoming hysterical and creating general unease on the flight and if not dealt with tactfully, the angry coach passenger may start shouting, storm off the coach and discourage other guests from attending another of your company's coach tours.

YOUR LOVE OF THE WORLD

As well as having the right skills and qualities to succeed in travel and tourism, it's also very helpful for many jobs to have a love and significant interest in the world around you and a genuine passion for travel.

You can show you have these interests by:

- Travelling as much as you can – and this includes the UK as well as abroad.

- Subscribe to and read travel magazines, as well as magazines like *National Geographic* which focus on the geography, wildlife and cultures of other countries.
- Visit galleries and museums that feature international exhibits which provide an insight into other countries. The Commonwealth Institute in London can be a good place to start.
- Sign up for courses and classes in anything related to the culture of other countries. This could be literally anything from Mexican cooking to Irish dancing.

- **Problem solving:** this is a very helpful skill to have when things go wrong or occur in an unexpected way. Clients and guests will understand that things do not always go to plan, but they will expect you to have a 'Plan B' to overcome any problems. So for example, a Transfer Representative will know exactly what to do should a client's luggage go missing or their taxi fail to show.
- **Report writing and IT:** many travel and tourism jobs require that reports be written up after a tour or season. Being able to write clearly and concisely and have good basic IT skills are vital for many roles, especially if incidents occur in holiday resorts or on tours.
- **Foreign languages:** if you want to work abroad, then having a skill in languages is extremely helpful and can help you provide a much better service to your guests or clients.
- **First aid:** having some basic first aid skills can be important when dealing with guests and clients with minor injuries. In some travel and tourism jobs, this is an essential skill to have.

QUIZ
Have you got the skills to make it in travel and tourism?

Answer the questions below to see if you have the skills that travel and tourism employers are looking for:

How do you most like to spend your weekend?

    a. With friends
    b. Playing sport
    c. Playing on my PC

Your boss at your Saturday job asks you to swap the till for stacking shelves. What next?

    a. Get to it – all experience is good experience
    b. Do it, reluctantly but to the best of my ability
    c. Do it as quickly as, maybe they'll let me off early?

Do you enjoy learning new languages?

    a. Yes! I am taking a language at A Level/S grade and want to learn more
    b. I did GCSE, it was fun and I know enough to get by
    c. Not really. Everybody speaks English anyway!

How do you prefer to communicate with people?

    a. Face-to-face
    b. On the telephone
    c. By text

You are supposed to babysit next Sunday but have just remembered you have an exam the next day. What do you do?

    a. Call in the help of a trustworthy mate who is looking for extra money
    b. Take your revision with you
    c. Apologise to the family but tell them you simply can't do it

A new teacher replaces one of your favourites. How do you react?

    a. Welcome them and look forward to getting to know a new member of staff
    b. I am polite but not overly friendly or chatty with them
    c. I don't really acknowledge them and keep myself to myself

Now tot up your scores. Do you have mainly As, Bs or Cs?

Mostly As – you are perfectly suited to a career in travel and tourism! You are a people-person willing to go the extra mile and somebody who copes well with unstructured days and sudden change. Your language skills will prove essential in this industry, as will your knack of solving problems fuss-free.

Mostly Bs – travel and tourism is definitely an industry you could consider entering. Your conversation language skills, bright telephone manner and love of sport could put you in good stead for either a role helping tourists on these shores, manning a tourist helpline or working at an activity holiday camp or ski resort.

Mostly Cs – travel and tourism is not the first career that is earmarked for you as you're a free spirit who often likes to go solo. Having said that, your independence and strength of character is the perfect combination for travelling the world alone – and then writing about your experiences on the go or when you get home!

THE PERSONAL QUALITIES

- **Cheerful and outgoing:** working with all sorts of people in all sorts of situations, you need to be able to put on a brave face, even when you are not feeling so good. Guests and clients will all want to be greeted by someone with a smile on their face.
- **Flexibility:** in the travel and tourism sector, things can change quickly and you need to be able to adjust as required. For example, you may find that you have to work unexpected bank holidays or work in Spain when you were expecting to be based in Portugal. Having a flexible approach will help make you popular with your employer.
- **Confidence:** this is an important quality to have. Guests and clients will be looking to you for guidance when abroad and need to feel that they can approach you should they have any problems while on a resort holiday, a special tour or if they become lost in a holiday centre or theme park.
- **Groomed appearance:** working in travel and tourism, you will need to be well turned out and have a clean and tidy appearance. In some cases, you may be required to wear a uniform. Wearing this with pride

is seen as important since you are representing your employer and also making yourself obvious to clients and guests.

- **Able to work under pressure:** things can often turn hectic in travel and tourism careers, so you need to be able to remain calm and stay in control. Once again, clients and guests will look to you when things go wrong and need to feel that all will be sorted soon so they have nothing to worry themselves about.
- **Stamina:** you may have to work long hours and many roles in the sector, such as Tour Guides, Holiday Centre and Theme Park Assistants, require that you spend long periods of time on your feet with few breaks. Travelling itself can also be tiring and jet lag may be an obstacle you need to get over quickly.
- **Healthy and resilient:** working overseas or very long hours, you need to have a good constitution and be able to cope with bad weather, unhappy guests and clients, troublesome timetables and stomach bugs.
- **Team working:** successful travel and tourism employees tend to be good team players. Working as a team is often essential for achieving the best results, especially when dealing with large groups or complicated itineraries.
- **Leadership:** associated with confidence, leadership is a key quality for Tour Guides and Tour Managers as well as Holiday Representatives and Cabin Crew. Tour Guides and Managers, for example, need to keep the attention of their clients and get them from A to B while Reps and Cabin Crew pass instructions on to passengers and clients.

QUIZ

Have you got the personal qualities you need to work in travel and tourism?

Is your personality perfect for making holidaymakers smile? Take this quiz and find out:

You're tired, irritable and on the bus. Somebody sits next to you and says, 'it's so warm out there, isn't it?' How do you respond?

    a. I agree and tell them the TV has forecast even more sun tomorrow
    b. Smile and say 'yeah'
    c. Quickly put your headphones in

The next day, on the same bus, you see an old lady struggle to sit down with her shopping bags. What do you do?

    a. Jump up to help her
    b. Wait a few minutes to see if anybody else helps before jumping up
    c. Nothing, sorry! I've had a hard day at school

How often do you watch the world news?

    a. Every day
    b. Occasionally
    c. Very rarely

You have been dying to see a certain movie for weeks but when you get there, the cinema is full. What do you do?

    a. See another movie
    b. Book tickets for the next day
    c. Storm off in a huff

You are completing a journalism project for media studies and you are required to interview a local MP. You have sent an e-mail to him/her but heard nothing. What do you do?

a. Send a follow-up e-mail. If there is still no response, telephone his/her secretary
b. Send a follow-up e-mail. If there is still no response, give up
c. Give up and find an alternative interviewee

The after-school club you are a member of is running an open evening and a teacher asks for somebody to co-ordinate the entire event. It's a big project, how do you respond?

a. Throw my hand up and volunteer
b. Ask a friend if they fancy sharing responsibility
c. Sit back... believing you'd mess it up

Now see how you did by adding up the letters your answers most matched up to.

Mostly As – you have the ideal personal qualities to make it in travel and tourism. You always have a ready smile and forever see the brighter side of life, perfect for bringing brightness into somebody's business trip or holiday. Giving up is never an option for you and you take responsibility easy – perfect for an industry which can be tough going and unpredictable.

Mostly Bs – you should definitely research careers in this industry. Friendliness, positivity, perseverance and a healthy interest in the world are a must, and while you're no stranger to any of these attributes, making the effort to exercise them regularly wouldn't go amiss!

Mostly Cs – whilst your travel and tourism attributes aren't totally up to scratch, it might be down to the fact you have little confidence in giving them a work out. You seem to avoid running to the rescue or taking on responsibility. This may be because you fear being rebuffed or a failure. You have the smile, the stamina and the ability to do any of the actions outlined in the questions, you just don't know it yet!

HOW TO DEVELOP THESE SKILLS AND QUALITIES

If the quizzes have reaffirmed your interest in a travel and tourism job, then developing the skills and qualities covered in this chapter could help kick start your chances. Take a look at the chart below for some ideas on how to do this for a number of these skills and qualities.

Skill or Quality	Ideas on how to get it
Customer facing	● Try to get some work experience or a part-time/summer job in a shop or café/restaurant. If you can, try an opening in a travel agents or holiday company. Your school may be able to help you this. Or try looking in a copy of the *Yellow Pages* for local employers.
Helpful and cheerful nature	● Help out at charity events ● Volunteer to work at the local hospital, children's or old person's home ● Join a conservation group ● Ask the organisations/people you help to write a short statement confirming this.

Continued on next page

Skill or Quality	Ideas on how to get it
First aid	• There are lots of first aid courses that you can take part time. The Scouts and Guides organisations often run courses as do St John's Ambulance. Your local Connexions office may be able to help you find a short, nearby course at a local college.
Foreign languages	• Consider taking a GCSE/S grade in a foreign language. Also consider other language options that you could do as a short/evening course. Request help locating such courses from your local Connexions office or from your school career adviser. Check out your local library too.
Stamina, resilience, responsibility	• Show you have staying power by sticking at the things you take on after school. So for example, if you get involved in some volunteering, try to remain committed to one project for at least a year • Likewise, with any school roles (such as prefect or librarian) you take on, try to keep the post for a couple of terms to show that you are both responsible and dedicated.

5

Case study 2

TRAVEL CONSULTANT

Sunburn, several thousand photos and tacky souvenirs… this is what most people bring back from their holidays. Not Anneka Fiske … she came home with a whole new career dream in her suitcase.

Six years ago, Anneka jetted in from a holiday in Thailand with one major goal – to set about securing a career in travel.

Anneka soon found work at Galaxy Travel as a Trainee Travel Consultant in Wisbech, East Anglia, where she juggled organising customers' far-flung journeys with studying for NVQs in Travel and Leisure Services through the TTC Travel Training Programme (TTP).

Before long, Anneka was made Travel Consultant and began to put her new-found skills into practice; making sun, snow and adventure seekers' holiday dreams come true. The course which saw Anneka fast-tracked through Galaxy had every aspect of her new role covered and helped boost her career confidence on the shop floor as well as her skills.

The shop floor is a place Anneka's skills now dominate; from banking and

> No two days are the same. One day I'll be helping people make a straightforward booking and the next I'll be helping people who aren't sure make the best choice for them.

authorising limited discounts on bookings to dealing with customer problems and conceiving creative ideas for new window displays.

'No two days are the same', says Anneka. 'One day I'll be helping people make a straight-forward booking and the next I'll be helping people who aren't sure make the best choice for them. It gives me a buzz to hear all about other places and then I can use that knowledge to do my job even better.'

Not only did Anneka reach the finals of the TTC's TTP Apprentice of the Year and win Galaxy Trainee of the Year ... she's now got her sights set on promotion to Senior Consultant and, in ten years time, manager.

But for now? 'I'm looking forward to my first taste of the Caribbean with a holiday to Jamaica next week!' says Anneka.

6

FAQs

Want to find out more about the travel and tourism jobs you've seen featured earlier in the book? Take a look at the FAQs – one for each job – to find out more about salaries, hours, entry routes and future prospects.

AIR CABIN CREW

- *How much will I get paid*? Starting salaries begin at around £10,000 to £12,000. Senior air cabin crew can earn around £25,000.
- *What will my hours be*? Hours are irregular as they fit in with flight schedules. Expect to work nights, weekends and public holidays.
- *Were will I work*? Mainly onboard planes in restricted space. Depending on the flights, you may be expected to spend long periods of time outside of the UK.
- *What do I need to get in*? Entry qualifications vary, but most airlines ask that applicants have a good number of GCSEs. English, Maths and a foreign language are helpful. Good health is essential. Airlines provide their own training which must be completed successfully in order to work on flights.
- *What are the perks*? You may be given flight and meal allowances. You can also earn commission for working on an agreed number of flights. Every now and then, you may be able to spend significant time in the countries you fly to.
- *Where can the job lead*? Prospects vary from airline to airline, but you could progress to become a purser and

so be responsible for a particular cabin, such as first or
business class. You could also move into ground work
and get involved in training or passenger related work.
There can also be opportunities to work overseas or
move into senior roles within flight or aircraft operations.

CRUISE SHIP WORK

- *How much will I get paid*? Salaries vary from cruise line
  to cruise line. First-timers may get around £400 a week.
  This should increase with experience.
- *What will my hours be*? These are likely to be long and
  variable. Expect to work weekends and bank holidays.
  Being onboard a ship 24/7, you may, in some cases, be
  almost constantly on call. Depending on the length of the
  cruise, you may be away from home for months at a time.
- *Where will I work*? Onboard cruise ships and often in
  ports of call too.
- *What do I need to get in*? Most reps on cruise ships
  have GCSEs which include Maths, English, Geography
  and a foreign language. A relevant qualification in travel
  and tourism is helpful. (See Chapter 7 'Training' for more
  detail.) You will also be expected to complete and pass a
  training course with your employer. Courses tend to last
  for around a month.
- *What are the perks*? You may find that you do not have
  to pay for meals or your cabin. You should be able to
  spend some time exploring your ports of call.
- *Where can the job lead*? You could move into
  management – managing the other representatives
  onboard ships. Or you could move into land-based
  office roles with your employer.

COACH TOUR OPERATOR

- *How much will I get paid*? The average starting salary is around £13,000 to £20,000. As a proven, experienced and successful operator you could expect your salary to increase to between £25,000 and £40,000 per annum.
- *What will my hours be*? They are likely to be varied. When researching and conducting office-based tasks, you'll probably work 9 to 5. On tour, your hours will be longer and you will be expected to work evenings, weekends and bank holidays.
- *Where will I work*? When office-based you will probably work in the UK. On tour, most coach trips will be in the UK or Europe, but you could work outside of Europe too.
- *What do I need to get in*? There are no formal requirements but most employees prefer people with degrees or HNDs in subjects such as travel and tourism, hotel/catering management, business related subjects, language related subjects, marketing, and IT.
- *What are the perks*? There are opportunities to travel and it is likely you would receive expenses for this travel.
- *Where can the job lead*? Opportunities vary from company to company. In bigger companies, you could move into senior management roles. Many tour operators go on to to set up their own agencies.

HOLIDAY REPRESENTATIVE

- *How much will I get paid*? At the start of their careers, holiday reps can earn around £400 to £500 per week. Salaries rise with experience and a proven track record.
- *What will my hours be*? There are no set hours but they tend to be long and will involve working evenings, weekends and bank holidays.

- *Where will I work*? This depends on where the resort you are working in is based – so quite literally, you could be working almost anywhere in the world.
- *What do I need to get in*? As a rule, the minimum age you need to be to become a holiday rep is 18 – although you will probably find that most employers look for candidates who are 21 plus. Qualifications wise, there are no set qualifications, but a good all round education is expected and many holiday reps have some GCSEs/S grades in English, Geography and Mathematics. However, should you choose to specialise in becoming a children's rep, you will need a qualification in nursery nursing such as a NNEB (National Nursery Examining Board) Diploma in Nursery Nursing or an NVQ Level 3 in Childcare as well as six months' experience working with children.
- *What are the perks*? Most holiday reps find their meals and accommodation paid for by their employer.
- *Where can the job lead*? Depending on the size of the company you work for, you could find promotion to a more senior position such as team leader or regional manager.

HOLIDAY CENTRE WORK

- *How much will I get paid*? Most holiday centre workers start with an average salary of £10,000. If you move into management, you could earn up to £30,000. You may receive tips and bonuses too.
- *What will my hours be*? Many holiday centre workers work around 40 hours a week. You would also be expected to work in the evenings and at weekends. Some holiday centre work is also seasonal.

- *Where will I work*? You will be based at the holiday centre that employs you and should expect to work both indoors and outdoors.
- *What do I need to get in*? There are no minimum entry requirements, but many workers, especially those involved in administrative duties, tend to have GCSEs/S levels in Maths and English. Vocational qualifications in leisure and tourism are also viewed favourably.
- *What are the perks*? There are often good training opportunities at many centres plus the option to specialise, such as working with children, outdoor sports and even hosting business events and conferences. Tips and bonuses can also add up to give your salary a significant boost.
- *Where can the job lead*? Prospects are often dictated by the size of company you join. Some of the bigger centres with branches around the UK may offer the opportunities to move into management roles. You could also choose to work in a holiday centre abroad – your UK work experience should go down well.

THEME PARK ASSISTANT

- *How much will I get paid*? The majority of starting salaries kick in at around £8,832. With some experience under your belt, you could find yourself earning around £10,000 a year.
- *What will my hours be*? Hours tend to be long – with a 40 hour week being pretty common. Since many theme parks are open everyday of the week, weekend work is required as is evening work. Shift work may be an option.
- *What do I need to get in*? There isn't a set standard but it is a legal requirement that operators of rides be at least

18 years old. Assistants on children's rides can start work at 16, though.

- *What are the perks*? You should receive on the job training and may be entitled to discounts on rides and attractions.
- *Where can the job lead*? With some experience and related training and depending on the size of theme park you work in, you could take up more supervisory roles and possibly specialise in related areas such as catering or security. You could also choose to work in major theme parks abroad such as Disneyland or Legoland.

TOUR GUIDE

- *How much will I get paid*? At the start of their careers, tour guides can earn around £10,000. With experience, salaries can increase to around £25,000. However, most tour guides are self-employed and find that their income varies depending on the amount of work they can get.
- *What will my hours be*? Hours are not generally fixed but long hours are the norm and depend on the length of the tour. Many guides find the work is seasonal and may work just during the summer months.
- *What do I need to get in*? No set qualifications are requested, but GCSEs/S grades are very useful, as is fluency in a foreign language. The Institute of Tourist Guiding (ITG) and the Scottish Tourist Guides Association (STGA) also offer guiding qualifications.
- *What are the perks*? You may receive discounts on related tours and will broaden your general knowledge. Some guides enjoy the seasonal aspect of the work and find they can experience other careers when not working in this area.

● *Where can the job lead*? Once experienced, you could become a trainer of other guides. It is also possible to move into tour operator work or travel agency work.

TOUR MANAGER

● *How much will I get paid*? Starting salaries tend to be around the £10,000 to £13,000 a year mark but do rise with experience. More experienced tour managers can earn around £25,000. Most tour managers are also freelance.

● *What will my hours be*? Typically, hours are long and tend to be irregular since you'll be with your group on tour pretty much 24/7. Expect to work evenings, weekends and bank holidays.

● *Where will I work*? Once on tour you could be based anywhere in the world. Basically, you go wherever your tour goes. You may spend some time in the office but most of the time you will be working away.

● *What do I need to get in*? There are no set requirements and many tour operators are more interested in the skills that people have rather than their exam results. However, having a foreign language is a definite advantage as is experience of working with people and being organised.

● *What are the perks*? You should find that your meals and accommodation are paid for. Most operators also pay for return flights to the destinations you are working in.

● *Where can the job lead*? As a freelancer, you could join a company and move up the ranks to become a tour operator or set up your own tour operations business.

TOURIST INFORMATION CENTRE ASSISTANT

- *How much will I get paid*? Salaries for this job vary from around £10,000 to £19,000 per year.
- *What will my hours be*? Typically, you will work office hours and probably be required to work Saturdays and bank holidays. Some smaller tourist information centres may only open during the summer months. Many jobs are part time.
- *Where will I work*? You will be office based in the centre of your choice. Expect work to be indoors.
- *What do I need to get in*? There are no formal requirements for this type of work but qualification in English and maths are well regarded as are qualification in history and geography. A foreign language is also an advantage.
- *What are the perks*? You can expect paid holidays and sick leave.
- *Where can the job lead*? Promotion can lead to senior and management roles.

TRANSFER REPRESENTATIVE

- *How much will I get paid*? A typical starting salary is around £10,000 per annum.
- *What will my hours be*? These are likely to be varied depending on when and where you are required to meet people. Expect evening, weekend and bank holiday work.
- *Where will I work*? This depends on the country you are based. You will probably spend time in an office and then time on the road travelling to meet clients at airports and the like.
- *What do I need to get in*? You don't need any specific qualifications but qualifications in maths, English and a

foreign language are good to have as is experience
working with people and being able to organise
yourself.

- *What are the perks*? You may find that your
  accommodation and meals are paid for.
- *Where can the job lead*? With a good track record, you
  could progress into more senior and also management
  roles.

TRAVEL AGENT SALES CONSULTANT

- *How much will I get paid*? As a trainee, you can expect
  to earn around £10,000. As you move up the ranks, you
  could earn around £30,000 a year.
- *What will my hours be*? Generally, you'll work a 35 to
  40 hour week, from 9 to 5 each day including Saturdays.
  If you work in a call centre you may also work Sundays
  and evenings as well as bank holidays.
- *Where will I work*? Most travel agents work either in a
  high street shop or in a call centre.
- *What do I need to get in*? There are no formal
  requirements, but having qualifications in maths and
  English is very helpful as is having a foreign language
  skill or a professional travel agent's qualification (see
  Chapter 7 for more details).
- *What are the perks*? Some companies offer their agents
  discounts on their holidays and bonus schemes for
  holidays sold. Some agents can work from home.
- *Where can the job lead*? You could progress fairly
  quickly into management or move into tour operations
  work. Some experienced travel agents set up their own
  agencies.

Training

The travel and tourism industry needs people with the right skills, personal qualities and qualifications. Many school leaver jobs in the sector state that they don't require a set standard entry requirement but it makes sense to get as many relevant qualifications as you can before you leave school or college and start your search for a travel or tourism job.

The good news is that there are plenty of related courses to choose from, with most of them being rated as Level 3 qualifications. This chapter looks at the sort of training and qualifications available for people looking for a career in travel and tourism.

WHAT COURSES ARE AVAILABLE?

From NVQ to degree level, most travel and tourism qualification are vocational and designed to help students develop the skills and knowledge that employers in the sector want and need. The table below should give you a good idea of what's available and directly related to travel and tourism.

DID YOU KNOW?

The people working in travel and tourism tend to be a pretty well qualified bunch. Around 80% of the work force is qualified to Level 4, Level 3 and Level 2. Only 5% have no qualifications.

Source: Labour Force Survey 2004q2–2005q1

Type of course	Entry requirements	Course description
Apprenticeships	There are a number of travel related apprenticeships available. There are not usually any set qualifications required for entry, but you do need to be over 16 years old and under 24 years old	This is a vocational qualification that combines 'earning and learning'. The emphasis is on the development of practical skills and knowledge. You will spend most of your time in a work situation but you will be required to spend time in college as well. You will also earn a wage while studying as well as other recognised vocational qualifications
GCSE: Leisure and Tourism	Entry requirements depend upon your school's or college's preferences	Usually taken at school and regarded as an academic qualification, GCSEs involve a mixture of academic study and some investigative work. Work is assessed through course work and exam. These courses last two years
Diploma: Travel and Tourism (from 2010)	Entry requirements depend upon your school's or college's preferences	Combining academic learning with hands-on practical skill development, diplomas can be taken at school or college. They provide a good introduction and insight into the sector that is assessed through course work and exams. Courses last for two years and some of this time may be spent in the workplace

Continued on next page

Type of course	Entry requirements	Course description
A Level: Travel and Tourism	Entry requirements depend upon your school's or college's preferences	Vocational A Levels like this can be taken at school or college and provide a broad overview of the travel and tourism sector. Assessment is a mixture of course work and final exam/s. Courses last for two years
BTEC First Diploma in Travel and Tourism	Most colleges ask for four GCSEs (grade A to G) or equivalent	BTECs are work-related qualifications that will involve some time spent learning and some time in a travel and tourism place of work where you will gain related skills and work experience. They are usually studied at college
BTEC National Diploma in Travel and Tourism	Expect to be asked for BTEC First Diploma in Travel and Tourism or a related subject, plus four GCSEs (grade A to C) or equivalent	This is a step up from the BTEC First Diploma, but is still a vocational qualification designed to equip you with the skills and knowledge prized by employers operating in the travel and tourism industry
NVQs/SVQs Levels 2, 3 and 4 in Travel Services	There are no set entry requirements	These are work-based qualifications that can be studied in some schools and colleges. Most of the learning is practical which enables you to develop the specific skills required by travel and tourism employers. These courses do not need to be completed within a specified amount of time

Continued on next page

Type of course	Entry requirements	Course description
SQA National Modules in Tourism or Travel and Tourism	Most institutions ask for four GCSEs/S grades (A–C/1–3) plus an A Level or two H grades or equivalent	Provided by the Scottish Qualifications Authority (SQA), these vocational modules can be studied for in Scottish institutions as part of the SQA National Certificate and Higher National Awards.
Higher National Certificate/ Diploma in Tourism or in Travel and Tourism	Entry requirements normally consist of four GSCEs/S grades (A–C/1–3), plus one A Level/two H grades or equivalent	Often described as a 'learning by doing' qualification, much of this qualification focuses on the practical aspects of working in travel and tourism. Expect assessment to be through coursework and exams. Full time, this course usually takes a year to complete
BTEC HNC/HND in Travel and Tourism Management	Expect to be asked for three GCSEs/S grades (A–C/1–3) which should include English and Mathematics. An A Level/two H grades or equivalent are also required	These are also work-based qualifications that concentrate on the development of skills relevant to working in travel and tourism. Mixing theory and practice, they are usually studied in college but can be studied in some schools in combination with GCSEs. Successful completion of the course could enable you to take a related higher education degree for a shorter time than normally required

Continued on next page

Type of course	Entry requirements	Course description
Foundation Degree	There are a number of travel and tourism Foundation Degrees available. There are no set entry requirements	You will spend a significant amount of time working in the travel and tourism sector gaining a practical insight into how the industry really works and gaining skills that related employers value. Most Foundation Degrees are assessed through a mixture of course work and exams. What you learn in the workplace will also be assessed. If completed successfully, a Foundation Degree could enable you to take a higher education degree in a shorter amount of time than normally required
Higher education degree in travel and tourism	Entry requirements vary from institution to institution but expect to have at least two A Levels/one S grade. Look out for courses affiliated to the ITT – the Institute of Travel and Tourism (see page 68 for details)	Studying this kind of vocational degree, you will spend time in the industry gaining specific work experience but you will also be required to write extended essays and complete project work. Most degree courses are assessed through the regular contribution of coursework rather than a big final exam
Related doctorate (postgraduate)	You will need to have a good quality higher education degree in a travel and tourism or related area	Expect there to be a lot of research involved as you put together a thesis on a certain area of travel and tourism. Much study time will be spent alone and most postgraduates take four to six years to complete their degree

FIND OUT MORE ABOUT...
- **Apprenticeships:** www.apprenticeships.co.uk and www.ttctraining.co.uk
- **GCSEs, NVQs/SNVQs, A Levels, Highers, BTECs:** www.city-and-guilds.co.uk; www.edexcel.org.uk; and www.ocr.org.uk
- **The new diploma:** www.people1st.co.uk/qualifications/qualification-reform/diploma-in-travel-and-tourism
- **Foundation and higher education degrees:** www.ucas.com
- **Professional qualifications:** www.ttctraining.co.uk

Don't forget to speak to your school's careers or Connexions adviser – they will be able to advise which of the courses mentioned in this chapter that you could study at school or in a local college.

OTHER COURSES
There are also courses that relate specifically to certain jobs in travel and tourism.

Air Cabin Crew
- BTEC Intermediate Certificate in Preparation for Air Cabin Crew.

Travel Agents/Tour Operators
- Fares and Ticketing Level 1
- Fares and Ticketing Level 2
- ABTAC British Travel Agents Certificate
- ABTA Certificate in Travel (tour operators).

General
- Passport into Travel.

WHICH COURSE IS RIGHT FOR YOU?

Reading this chapter, you'll have noticed that there is no one set travel or tourism qualification that can guarantee you a related job. So, you need to be sure that you pick the right course for the job you hope to get. For example, there is no point taking an Air Cabin Crew qualification if you really want to work as a Holiday Representative.

Consider the tips below before deciding on a course:

- Call up the personnel office of any future employers you are hoping to work for and ask them what qualifications they like their employees to have
- Ask teachers or college staff which courses match to the travel and tourism career you hope to have
- If you can, talk to ex-students about the courses they took and find out if the course helped them get the jobs they were after
- When considering courses, look at the amount of course work to work experience ratio – you may find some employers favour students who have taken more practical courses and vice versa.

DID YOU KNOW?

That if you work in travel and tourism, you're more likely to receive more training than people working in other industries. A recent Labour Force Survey revealed that 26% of people working in travel and tourism services received related training beneficial to their jobs in the last 13 weeks – in other industries only 23% of the work force had had any training.

Source: LFS, 2004q2–2005q1

8

Case study 3

TOUR MANAGER

After studying at a university in the north of England for three years, Ben Evans walked away with a good degree in travel and tourism. Here we find out how he went on to work as a self employed tour manager.

'I've always had a passion for travel,' says Ben, 'right from childhood, I'd say. So I guess I was one of the lucky ones at school who knew just what that they wanted to do career wise – work in travel and tourism.'

As one of the 'lucky ones', Ben, sure of the fact that he wanted to work in the travel and tourism industry, explored the options available to him. Being relatively academic, Ben took six GCSEs and two A Levels which included Geography and Spanish. He also gained some work experience in a travel agent and spent six months in Spain before he took his place up at university.

'Although I knew the industry I wanted to work in,' reveals Ben, 'it took me a while to decide which job I actually wanted to pursue. The work experience I had was

I think having a degree helped, but it is not essential for working in this line.

enjoyable but it made me realise that I didn't want to sell holidays – I wanted to be a part of them – which is why tour management seemed right for me. In his role I would be out and about both experiencing and showing people how wonderful other countries are.'

Once graduated, Ben returned to Spain for some travelling. Being able to speak Spanish fluently, Ben was able to get on with local people, learn more about the country and discover attractions off the beaten track.

Ben says, 'Having spent a fair bit of time in Spain, I came to really love the place. So once I returned to the UK, I started approaching tour companies operating in Spain. On my CV, I made it clear that I knew the country well and that I was qualified to speak the language. My work experience demonstrated I could work with people. I think having a degree helped, but it is not essential for working in this line.'

A few weeks after sending in his CV on spec, Ben was having interviews and in a short while was offered a contract to work in Spain as a tour manager in the south of the country. 'It's great,' comments Ben. 'I get to work in a country I love and meet people from all over. The hours are long and being self-employed means I sometimes have times when I don't work, but I wouldn't change my line of work for anything.'

Action plans

Match the job you are interested in to one of the action plans below. Each plan suggests activity ideas that will help your CV stand out should you interview for such a role in the future. Tick off each activity in the 'Achieved' box as you work through them. Don't forget to add these achievements to your CV!

TRAVEL AGENT SALE CONSULTANT

Things to do	Achieved
Get an atlas and familiarise yourself with the world's continents, countries and major cities	
Buy and read travel magazines and the travel sections in newspapers	
Visit as many places as possible – in the UK as well as abroad	
Log on to travel company websites and see what kind of packages are on offer. Look to see how different travel agencies specialise in certain packages or clientele	
When you visit places, write down the memorable things you enjoyed	
Enquire about foreign exchange trips at school to sample another culture and flex those language skills	
Get work experience or a summer job in a travel agent's – or take on a role that will exercise your administration skills	
Consider learning a second language, even if it is just to conversational level	
Join the drama or debating club and give those communication skills a good workout	
Exercise your IT skills daily	
Research travel and tourism qualifications at your local college	
Speak to somebody who has had experience in this field, and ask them 'what skills do you wish you'd packed in your suitcase?' – their answer will be invaluable!	

AIR CABIN CREW

Things to do	Achieved
Study for a second language either at school or out-of-hours	
Learn as much as you can about other countries and cultures; by reading books, watching movies and surfing the internet	
Secure work experience in an air travel-related role, i.e. a travel agency or airline information desk at an airport	
If the above is not possible, choose a placement that exercises your communication and customer service skills to the max	
Take a Saturday job in a shop or café – superb experience for those forthcoming duties in the sky	
Volunteer helping elderly or young people – the responsibility that comes with assisting the vulnerable and ability to get on with folks from all walks of life will give your CV a definite edge	
Attend drama classes – they're a great way to develop your communication skills	
Enquire about foreign exchange trips at school to sample another culture and flex those language skills	
Visit airline websites and study the routes they specialise in and decide whether domestic or international flights are for you	
Take a course in first aid – essential on board and highly transferrable into other industries	
Consider joining the St John's Ambulance Brigade – dealing with attendees of a festival or event who've fainted is the perfect way to prepare you for 33,000ft dilemmas!	
School presidency up for grabs? Captain needed for the running team? Go for it and work those leadership skills	
Speak to somebody who has had experience in this field, and ask them 'what skills do you wish you'd packed in your suitcase?' – their answer will be invaluable!	

CRUISE SHIP WORK

Things to do	Achieved
Work those sea legs! From the local ferry to a school trip to Calais – floating life can take some getting used to	
Decide which area of ship life you'd like to specialise in and grab as much experience as you can relating to it – think catering, entertainment or perhaps even childminding	
Take a first aid course – it's essential	
Find a Saturday job that brings you face-to-face with your public... and practise that smile (it will soothe those sea-phobes later in life)	
If a water-related role is out of reach, think customer service, communication and organisational placements	
Whether it's the netball or football team, the school magazine or drama club; team work experience is essential offshore as you'll be living as well as working with your close colleagues!	
Buy and read travel magazines and the travel sections in newspapers	
Travel! It doesn't have to be to exotic shores, it could be the next city... but a passion for seeing other worlds (no matter how small) strengthens your industry candidacy	
Keep travel journals outlining your out-of-town or overseas adventures	
Research travel and tourism qualifications at your local college	
Speak to somebody who has had experience in this field, and ask them 'what skills do you wish you'd packed in your suitcase?' – their answer will be invaluable!	

COACH TOUR MANAGER

Things to do	Achieved
Travel as much as you can – by coach, boat or plane	
Buy and read travel magazines and the travel sections in newspapers	
Write notes on your new adventures and reveal what you liked most about new towns/countries	
Invite a friend from out of town and take them on a tour of your city	
Take an active interest in the drama or debating club at school – learning to speak confidently and animatedly to others ... nerve free!	
Ask a local tour company whether you can 'sit in' on one of their guided tours	
Better still, ask them for work experience	
Whether it's captain of a sports team or childminding your neighbours brood – responsibility and leadership are tour manager essentials	
Do karaoke! Getting used to working a microphone is easier than it looks!	
Research travel and tourism qualifications at your local college	
Speak to somebody who has had experience in this field, and ask them 'what skills do you wish you'd packed in your suitcase?' – their answer will be invaluable!	

HOLIDAY REPRESENTATIVE

Things to do	Achieved
Learn a second language – at school if possible or in your own time	
Buy and read travel magazines and the travel sections in newspaper	
Try writing your own mini features on places you've been to – even if it's only the a trip to the local beach	
Volunteer for a role that offers responsibility and requires supervising others – think coaching sport to younger children or teaching drama	
Alternatively, help out at a local youth club or even an old people's home and help organise summer day trips out	
Find a Saturday job that entails offering others advice face to face or answer enquiries on the telephone	
Look for a role that is customer-service driven and will give you hands-on problem solving experience	
Exercise your independence! Travelling abroad will mean leaving behind everything and everyone that is familiar – tackle projects solo or take a day trip out alone	
Similarly, strengthen your team working skills. Working for the school magazine (see below) is ideal	
Enrol in drama classes or sign up as a reporter for the school magazine – any extra-curricular activity that boosts communication skills and involves social interaction	
Enquire about foreign exchange trips at school to sample another culture and flex those language skills	
Sign up for a first aid course	
Research travel and tourism qualifications at your local college	
Speak to somebody who has had experience in this field, and ask them 'what skills do you wish you'd packed in your suitcase?' – their answer will be invaluable!	

HOLIDAY CENTRE WORKER

Things to do	Achieved
Stay in one! Even if it means begging the old folks to shun the 5* hotel!	
Café, shop or cleaning work may not be your dream weekend activity but the skills picked up never go out of fashion in holiday centres	
Try and secure work experience in a holiday camp over summer	
Do you want to cook, sing or play ball in the pool with kids? Pick your passion, and get the practice in asap	
Volunteer for a role supervising those younger people – think sport, drama or art	
Enquire about foreign exchange trips at school to sample another culture and flex those language skills	
Take a first aid course	
Editor of the school magazine or captain of the swimming team – if a leadership role is up for grabs, grab it	
Research travel and tourism qualifications at your local college	
Speak to somebody who has had experience in this field, and ask them 'what skills do you wish you'd packed in your suitcase?' – their answer will be invaluable!	

THEME PARK ASSISTANT

Things to do	Achieved
Visit theme parks as much as you can over the summer holidays – and decide which area you'd prefer to work in	
If you can't find a summer job at a theme park, think cafés, shops or local leisure centres...	
And think cash! Cash-handling skills are essential in theme parks	
Volunteer for a role supervising children – theme parks' biggest fans!	
Visit British tourist board websites and see what the world is saying about our resorts and attractions	
Sign up for a first aid course	
Research health and safety legislations surrounding theme parks and funfairs	
Never say no to the biggest, fastest ride at a resort	
Keep fit and active to prepare for this busy career	
Speak to somebody who has had experience in this field, and ask them 'what skills do you wish you'd packed in your suitcase?' – their answer will be invaluable!	

TOUR GUIDE

Things to do	Achieved
Learn a second language, or even a third	
Take local tours and speak with the guides working on them	
Wherever you holiday, book yourself onto the tours available to visitors	
Never walk on when a tourist stops you for directions or information	
Don't sit at the back of the drama class, make yourself heard and be confident!	
Consider taking speech and drama exams (LAMDA, Guildhall...)	
Volunteer for a role that includes both organisational and leadership elements; local groups for disabled children are excellent as you could take responsibility for organising a fun day out for them	
Saturday jobs in anything from a pet shop to a fast-food restaurant will strengthen customer service skills	
Enquire about foreign exchange trips at school to sample another culture and flex those language skills	
Write local travel pieces for the school magazine or website	
Take a first aid course	
Research travel and tourism qualifications at your local college	
Speak to somebody who has had experience in this field, and ask them 'what skills do you wish you'd packed in your suitcase?' – their answer will be invaluable!	

TOUR MANAGER

Things to do	Achieved
Take local tours and when you book, talk to the company about the service they provide	
Wherever you holiday, book yourself onto the tours available to visitors	
Scour tour operator websites and research the many different types of tours on offer	
Devise your own local ghost or music tour and invite your mates	
Volunteer for a role that includes both organisational and leadership elements; organise a new music fundraising night or a sponsored run past the town's tourist hot spots	
Never step away from responsibility; whether at school or in your Saturday job	
Consider an administrative part-time job or one which involves answering enquiries from the public	
Write local travel pieces for the school magazine or website – you never know when you'll be asked to step into the guide's absent shoes!	
Take a first aid course	
Research travel and tourism qualifications at your local college	
Speak to somebody who has had experience in this field, and ask them 'what skills do you wish you'd packed in your suitcase?' – their answer will be invaluable!	

TOUR OPERATOR

Things to do	Achieved
Whenever and wherever there's a tour – take it!	
Devise a series of summer tours and invite friends and family – consider 'employing' some of them as guides too!	
Create mini brochures or e-shots promoting your tours or ask a friend and manage them through the project	
Tours a big success? Place an ad in the local free paper, and invite more people along!	
School trip in the offing? Ask if you can help organise it!	
Start enquiring about work experience at a tour operating company immediately	
Learn a second language at least to conversational level	
Endeavour to secure a voluntary role that will stretch your organisational ability – organise a charity fashion show from scratch or a sponsored footy match featuring a local soap celeb	
Visit tour operators websites – from the most famous to the most obscure	
Research travel and tourism qualifications at your local college	
Speak to somebody who has had experience in this field, and ask them 'what skills do you wish you'd packed in your suitcase?' – their answer will be invaluable!	

TOURIST INFORMATION CENTRE ASSISTANT

Things to do	Achieved
Visit your local town or city centre; browse, ask questions, pick up leaflets. If you realise you don't know your city well, get to know it ... fast!	
Learn a second language and research the cultures of the tourists who mainly visit your town or city	
Secure part-time work in a role that involves assisting others with problems/enquiries, e.g. shop or museum/gallery assistant	
Research work experience – if not in an information centre itself – that flexes your problem-solving skills, e.g. lost property office or ticket desk at a station	
Volunteer for a charity which offers a helpline/advice desk	
Never overlook the opportunity to offer directions to visitors in town	
Travel and visit new places as much as possible	
Keep a travel diary that recalls the highlights of your journeys	
Write a list of 100 things you adore about your hometown	
Enquire about foreign exchange trips at school to sample another culture and flex those language skills	
Be a leader! Coach younger years in swimming or practise improvisational skills with the Year 7 drama club	
Research travel and tourism qualifications at your local college	
Speak to somebody who has had experience in this field, and ask them 'what skills do you wish you'd packed in your suitcase?' – their answer will be invaluable!	

TRANSFER REPRESENTATIVE

Things to do	Achieved
Learn at least one other language and know the basics in several	
Travel and travel some more, whenever the opportunity arises	
Want to stay home? Get to know your hometown and everything it has to offer	
Want to travel? Pick a country or continent and begin an ongoing research project into everything from its culture to its best hotels	
Find part-time work – such as working in a shoe store – that stretches your ability to advice and offer opinion and boost the wellbeing of the customer	
Secure work experience at an airport for a tour operator or airline	
If the above is not possible, consider hotel work especially on reception	
Volunteer to help on a day out/break for local children or disabled adults, offering to take responsibility for locating the hotel, finding the cheapest café etc	
Take speech and drama exams (LAMDA, Guildhall...) speaking with confidence and authority is the key to this career	
Enquire about foreign exchange trips at school to sample another culture and flex those language skills	
Work with animals or learn sign language – this seemingly obscure experience will work in your favour when the pet-carrying or hard-of-hearing passenger flies in	
Keep fit and healthy – you never know when case-carrying duties will call	
Promise to never leave the house looking anything less than well-groomed... and build up that business wardrobe	
Research travel and tourism qualifications at your local college	
Speak to somebody who has had experience in this field, and ask them 'what skills do you wish you'd packed in your suitcase?' – their answer will be invaluable!	

10

The last word

Now that you've reached this chapter, you'll have found out a significant amount about careers in travel and tourism. You've found out that there are a large number of varied jobs available in the sector all needing people with distinct qualifications, personal qualities and skills.

However, although the jobs may be varied there are common themes that bind travel and tourism careers together. And that's an interest in the world around you, a love of working for and with people as well as energy, commitment and a willingness to work hard. If you have these attributes then you're half way to getting your dream travel and tourism job already.

Mix this with some relevant work experience or volunteering opportunity and the right course and your CV will really shine out to prospective employers in the sector. Take the time to make sure the role you are interested in is right for you and you could have a career in travel and tourism that could not only take you around the world, but be one that motivates and satisfies you for a lifetime.

Now that you've made it this far through the book, it's time to see if a career in travel and tourism is really for you. Take a look at the checklist below to see if you have chosen wisely.

THE LAST WORD ✔ TICK YES OR NO

DO YOU HAVE A LOVE OF THE WORLD AND ALL ITS AMAZING COUNTRIES AND PEOPLES?
☐ YES
☐ NO

DO YOU ENJOY WORKING WITH PEOPLE?
☐ YES
☐ NO

ARE YOU FIT, HEALTHY AND RESILIENT?
☐ YES
☐ NO

ARE YOU WILLING TO WORK LONG HOURS AND AT WEEKENDS?
☐ YES
☐ NO

DO YOU BELIEVE THE CUSTOMER IS ALWAYS RIGHT?
☐ YES
☐ NO

ARE YOU AS HAPPY AWAY FROM HOME AS YOU ARE AT HOME?
☐ YES
☐ NO

ARE YOU CHEERFUL BY NATURE?
☐ YES
☐ NO

DO YOU WANT TO WORK IN AN INDUSTRY THAT'S FAST MOVING AND EVER-CHANGING?
☐ YES
☐ NO

If you answered 'YES' to all these questions then CONGRATULATIONS! YOU'VE CHOSEN THE RIGHT CAREER! If you answered 'NO' to any of these questions then this may not be the career for you. However, if you are still keen to work in the sector, there are related jobs such as IT and accounting (see page x for more details) which could enable you to still have involvement in the industry.

11

Further information

TRAVEL ORGANISATIONS

ABTA (Association of British Travel Agents)
68–71 Newman Street
London
W1T 3AH
Tel: 020 7637 2444
Web: www.abta.com

AITO (Association of Independent Tour Operators)
133A St Margaret's Road
Twickenham
TW1 1RG
Tel: 020 8744 9280
Web: www.aito.co.uk

CIMTIG (Chartered Institute of Marketing Travel
Industry Group)
c/o CIM
Moor Hall
Cookham
Maidenhead
S16 9QH
Tel: 01628 427500
Web: www.cimtig.org

GTMC (Guild of Travel Management Companies)
Queens House
180–182 Tottenham Court Road
London
W1T 7PD
Tel: 020 7637 1091
Web: www.gmtc.org

Irish Travel Agents Association
Heaton House
32 South William Street
Dublin 2
Eire
Tel: +353 1 679 4179
Web: www.itaa.ie

NAITA (National Association of Independent Travel Agencies)
Kenilworth House
79–80 Margaret Street
London
W1N 7HB
Tel: 020 7323 3408
Web: www.advantage4travel.com

Tourism Trade Organisation
Thames Tower
Black's Road
London
W6 9EL
Tel: 020 8846 9000
Web: www.tourismtrade.org.uk

World Tourism Organisation
Capitán Haya 42
28020 Madrid
Spain
Tel: +34 91 567 81 00
Web: www.unwto.org

HELPFUL TRAINING/SKILLS ORGANISATION
ITT (Institute of Travel and Tourism)
PO Box 217
Ware
SG12 8WY
Tel: 0844 4995 653
Web: www.itt.co.uk

People 1st
2nd Floor
Armstrong House
38 Market Square
Uxbridge
UB8 1LH
Tel: 0870 060 2550
Web: www.people1st.co.uk

Springboard UK
3 Denmark Street
London
WC2H 8LP
Tel: 020 7497 8654
Web: www.springboarduk.org.uk

Become instantly more attractive

To employers and further education providers
Whether you want to be an architect (Construction and
the Built Environment Diploma); a graphic designer
(Creative and Media Diploma); an automotive engineer
(Engineering Diploma); or a games programmer (IT
Diploma), we've got a Diploma to suit you. By taking our
Diplomas you'll develop essential skills and gain insight
into a number of industries. Visit our website to see
the 17 different Diplomas that will be available to you.
www.diplomainfo.org.uk

Travel Training Company
The Quayside
4 Furnival Road
Sheffield
S4 7YA
Tel: 0800 915 9396
Web: www.ttctraining.co.uk

RELATED LEARNING AND CAREER INFORMATION

CACHE (Council for Awards in Children's Care and Education)
Beaufort House
Grosvenor Road
St Albans
AL1 3AW
Tel: 01727 818616
Web: www.cache.org.uk

CILT (Centre for Information on Language Teaching
and Research)
20 Bedfordbury
London
WC2N 4LB
Tel: 020 7379 5101
Web: www.cilt.org.uk

National Council for the Training of Journalists
The New Granary
Station Road
Newport
Saffron Walden
CB11 3PL
Tel: 01799 544014
Web: nctj.com

Qualifications and Curriculum Authority
83 Piccadilly
London
W1J 8QA
Tel: 020 7509 5555
Web: www.qca.org.uk

UCAS (Universities and Colleges Admissions Service)
PO Box 28
Cheltenham
GL52 3LZ
Tel: 01242 222444
Web: www.ucas.com

HELPFUL MAGAZINES

Coach Monthly
Web: www.cdc-coachmonthly.co.uk

Conference and Incentive Travel
Web: www.Citmagazine.com

Green Tourism
Web: www.euromediaal.com/green.html

Group Travel Organiser
Web: www.grouptravelorganiser.com

Incentive Travel and Corporate Meetings
Web: www.incentivetravel.co.uk

Travel Weekly
Web: www.travelweekly.co.uk

Travel Mole (online news)
Web: www.travelmole.com

HELPFUL PUBLICATIONS

Careers Uncovered: Travel Industry, Sara Evans
(Trotman, 2006)
ISBN: 978 1 84455 105 7

Getting into Toursim, Verite Reily Collins (Trotman, 2006)
ISBN: 978 0 85660 459 1

How to get ahead in Leisure and Tourism (Trotman, 2006)
ISBN: 978 1 40620 447 6

Working on Cruise Ships, Sandra Bow (Trotman, 2006)
ISBN: 978 1 854583383

Careers and Jobs in Travel and Tourism, Verite Reily
Collins (Kogan Page Ltd 2004)
ISBN: 978 0749442057

Global Travel-Tourism Career Opportunities, G. E. Mitchell
(Booksurge Llc, 2006)
ISBN: 978 0945439141

Working in Travel and Tourism (My Future Career),
Margaret McAlpine (Gareth Stevens Publishing, 2004)
ISBN: 978 0836842395

Careers in Travel, Tourism, & Hospitality, 2nd edition
Marjorie Eberts, Linda Brothers, and Ann Gisler
(McGraw-Hill Contemporary, 2006)
ISBN: 978 0071448567

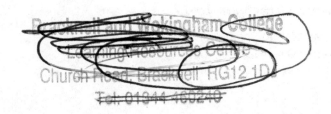